@RosenTeenTalk

PTSD

Kathleen A. Klatte

Published in 2024 by The Rosen Publishing Group, Inc.
2544 Clinton Street, Buffalo, NY 14224

First Edition

Editor: Greg Roza
Designer: Rachel Rising

Photo Credits: Cover, pp. 1, 4, 5, 45 TheVisualsYouNeed/Shutterstock.com; Cover, pp. 1–48 Vitya_M/Shutterstock.com; Cover Cosmic_Design/Shutterstock.com; pp. 3, 21 Photology1971/Shutterstock.com; pp. 3, 31 dekazigzag/Shutterstock.com; pp. 3, 39 Gingo Scott/Shutterstock.com; pp. 3, 43 logoboom/Shutterstock.com; p. 6 Trueffelpix/Shutterstock.com; p. 7 Jinitzail Hernandez/Shutterstock.com; p. 8 Daoduangnan/Shutterstock.com; p. 9 Enlightened Media/Shutterstock.com; p. 10 tadamichi/Shutterstock.com; p. 11 fizkes/Shutterstock.com; p. 13 Robert Crum/Shutterstock.com; p. 15 InfinitumProdux/Shutterstock.com; p. 17 cheapbooks/Shutterstock.com; p. 19 Drazen Zigic/Shutterstock.com; p. 23 Gorodenkoff/Shutterstock.com; p. 24 R. MACKAY PHOTOGRAPHY, LLC/Shutterstock.com; p. 25 Pixel-Shot/Shutterstock.com; p. 26 enterlinedesign/Shutterstock.com; p. 27 Golden Pixels LLC/Shutterstock.com; p. 27 Jullius/Shutterstock.com; p. 28 Panuwach/Shutterstock.com; p. 29 Mangostar/Shutterstock.com; p. 32 melitas/Shutterstock.com; p. 33 Prostock-studio/Shutterstock.com; p. 34 Wetzkaz Graphics/Shutterstock.com; p. 35 Zorro Stock Images/Shutterstock.com; p. 37 Anthony Correia/Shutterstock.com; p. 41 digitalskillet/Shutterstock.com; p. 42 Irina Strelnikova/Shutterstock.com.

Some of the images in this book illustrate individuals who are models. The depictions do not imply actual situations or events.

Library of Congress Cataloging-in-Publication Data

Names: Klatte, Kathleen A., author.
Title: PTSD / Kathleen A. Klatte.
Other titles: Post-traumatic stress disorder
Description: [New York, NY] : Rosen Publishing, [2024] | Series:
  @RosenTeenTalk | Includes bibliographical references and index.
Identifiers: LCCN 2022058301 (print) | LCCN 2022058302 (ebook) | ISBN
  9781499469318 (library binding) | ISBN 9781499469301 (paperback) | ISBN
  9781499469325 (ebook)
Subjects: LCSH: Post-traumatic stress disorder--Juvenile literature.
Classification: LCC RC552.P67 K577 2024 (print) | LCC RC552.P67 (ebook) |
  DDC 616.85/21--dc23/eng/20221214
LC record available at https://lccn.loc.gov/2022058301
LC ebook record available at https://lccn.loc.gov/2022058302

Manufactured in the United States of America

CPSIA Compliance Information: Batch #CSRYA24. For Further Information contact Rosen Publishing at 1-800-237-9932.

Find us on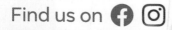

CONTENTS

Chapter 1

What Is PTSD?

I didn't want to come to school today. I had another nightmare about a shooting at a school in my state. My cousin goes to that school. She's okay, but has friends who died. I told my mom I have a stomachache, but she said I had to come to school anyway because I have missed too many days.

My school put in **metal detectors** and there are police. It's supposed to be safe, but it feels more like a jail than school. There's an active shooter drill planned for this afternoon. My friend Jaz's parents got her a bulletproof backpack. Why? We're not in the army! Why should we have to worry about stuff like this?

And what difference does it make? How can someone just get a gun and go to a school and shoot people? It doesn't make sense.

> Lots of kids were scared to go to school after a terrible shooting at Robb Elementary School in Uvalde, Texas, in 2022. Lots of parents were scared to send their kids to school too.

BREAKING IT DOWN

PTSD stands for post-traumatic stress disorder. It's a long-term **reaction** to a very scary or **dangerous** event. PTSD can affect people who were involved in the event or saw it happen. Some events are bad enough that people who weren't there are affected.

PTSD can cause people to relive a terrible event in bad dreams. It can make people feel sad or angry. They might be scared even when they are not in danger.

POST   TRAUMATIC   STRESS   DISORDER

Word Wisdom

post-: A prefix that means "after."

traumatic: Having to do with trauma. Trauma can mean a serious injury, or harm, to the body. It can also mean the feelings that result from an injury or scary event.

stress: Something that causes strong feelings of worry.

disorder: A condition that affects the body (physical) or the mind (mental).

The school where a terrible shooting occurred will often be torn down. That way, students who could experience PTSD don't ever have to go there again.

DEPRESSION

PTSD is a **complicated** condition. Sometimes people who live with PTSD also have other disorders. One of these is depression.

No matter how upset you are, it's important to remember you're never alone. Find a trusted adult to talk to if your feelings are too much to handle by yourself.

It's normal to be upset after something bad happens. When someone is feeling sad, worthless, or alone a long time after the bad event has passed, they may be living with depression. Depression is a medical condition. It can be treated with **therapy** or sometimes medicine, or drugs.

SIGNS OF DEPRESSION IN TEENS

- Sleeping too much or too little
- Feeling grumpy
- Acting out
- Weight loss or gain
- Unexplained illness
- Loss of interest in hobbies
- Inability to pay attention in school

ANXIETY

Anxiety can also be part of PTSD. Anxiety is a fear that something bad might happen. Sometimes there's no reason for that fear. When the movie *Jaws* came out, people were afraid to go swimming, even though actual shark attacks are very rare!

If you've seen something terrible in the news, it's natural to be afraid that it might happen to you too. When that fear lasts for a long time, or **interferes** with your life, it's time to ask for help.

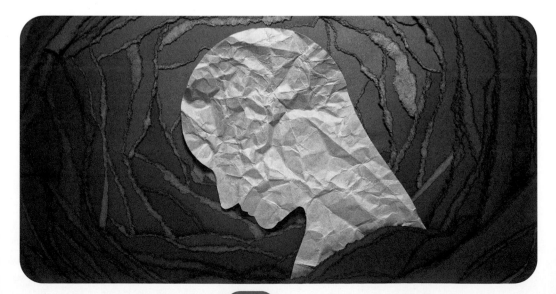

There's Help

Are you nervous to talk about your anxiety with loved ones? You can connect with a **counselor** at any time. Text HOME to 741741. Find out more at crisistextline.org.

People who feel alone are more likely to live with PTSD. It's important to share your worries with a trusted adult. They can help you figure out the best way to deal with your feelings.

MORE THAN A MINOR CRASH

I'm still shaking.

The school bus got into a fender bender, or small crash, this morning. Nobody got hurt. Everyone says it's no big deal. They're even making jokes about being late for school. I know they're right, but I'm still freaked out.

I was in a really bad car crash with my folks a few years ago. The car turned over. My dad and I got out, but my mom was trapped inside. The people who arrived in an ambulance got her out and she was okay, but I still have bad dreams about that day.

Even though no one got hurt today, the sound of metal crunching and the feeling of the bus being hit took me right back to the crash.

Sometimes, something minor, or small, can trigger, or cause, a big reaction. This reaction is often connected to a scary past event, even one that happened a long time ago.

FLASHBACKS

Flashbacks can be a symptom, or sign, of PTSD. A flashback is a very strong memory of something that happened to you. Some flashbacks are so strong that you might think you're reliving the event. You might also forget where you are. Flashbacks can be triggered by a sound or a smell. They can also be brought on by seeing a news story similar to your own bad experience.

WHAT IS SEXUAL ASSAULT?

Sexual assault happens when someone touches another person in a sexual way without their permission, or okay. It is also when someone forces another to participate in a sexual activity. Someone who's been sexually assaulted might be triggered by a sight, sound, touch, or smell that reminds them of their attacker.

What Is a Trigger?

A trigger is something that causes a strong **emotional** response. It can be something like a sound or smell.

The sound or smell of fireworks can be scary to someone who's experienced gun violence. "Violence" means using force to harm someone.

NIGHTMARES

PTSD often involves major sleep problems. Sleep is important to the health of your mind and body. After a scary event, it's natural to have bad dreams or even nightmares. You may have trouble falling asleep. Without enough sleep, you feel tired. You have trouble thinking clearly and remembering things. You might also be cranky.

It's important to talk to a trusted adult if you're having trouble sleeping. Sometimes you can talk through the problem. You might need help from a doctor. Not getting enough rest can affect your grades.

Not getting enough rest isn't healthy. It can make you too tired for fun things like playing sports. Being too tired makes it more likely you could get hurt.

HOW LONG IS LONG TERM?

It's normal to be upset or have bad dreams after something scary happens. For many people, these symptoms will fade quickly. For others, bad feelings can last longer. If someone is still scared or not sleeping well a month or more after the event, they might be living with PTSD.

If you're having trouble doing everyday things weeks after an upsetting event, it's time to ask for help. Only a doctor can correctly **diagnose** PTSD. They can refer you to a specialist who works with survivors of terrible events.

> It can be scary to return to the place where a bad thing happened, such as school, work, or the store. It's all right if you need to work with a doctor to get back to doing normal activities.

Chapter 2

What Causes PTSD?

Dad yelled at me again this morning. He's been really cranky since he started working overnights. At first, Mom said we needed to be quiet so he could get enough sleep.

But now I think there's something else going on. I heard Mom talking on the phone with Papa. There's a gang or something robbing 24-hour gas stations and stores around here. Dad's boss told him his other store was robbed last week and the clerk was injured. The police are trying to catch them, but there are a lot of places that are open all night. My folks are scared that Dad's place might be hit next.

I wish he could work someplace else. I don't like that Mom and Dad are scared all the time. It makes me scared too.

People who work alone at night may worry about being robbed or hurt if they know someone such as a coworker who has been harmed on the night shift. Over time, this can develop into PTSD.

SUDDEN EVENTS

PTSD can be caused by experiencing sudden events such as accidents, **disasters**, or attacks. PTSD can also be caused by things like **abuse** or **neglect** that take place over a long time.

Often there is lots of help available after a major event. This is usually true if it was in the news. Your school or the government might provide counseling and other services. People who don't have a strong support network are more likely to live with PTSD.

WHO CAN I TALK TO?

- Parent
- Teacher
- School Counselor
- Coach

- A Friend's Parent
- Older Sibling
- A Family Friend
- Religious Leader

Get Help

You can get facts and **resources** about PTSD from the National Center for PTSD. Check out their website: www.ptsd.va.gov.

Often counselors help first responders, such as firefighters and police, after a terrible **tragedy**. It's never a sign of weakness to need help.

DANGEROUS JOBS

When someone mentions PTSD, what's the first kind of person you think of? It's probably a soldier. A soldier who has been in **combat** may have been shot at by enemies. They may have had explosives go off near them. They may have been badly hurt or seen their friends die.

COMBAT VETERAN LIVES HERE

Please Be Courteous With

FIREWORKS

Or maybe you thought of a first responder. Firefighters and police officers experience terrible things in their careers, or jobs. Doctors used to think that only people who experienced trauma firsthand could be diagnosed with PTSD.

Fireworks aren't fun for everyone. The noise can be very upsetting for a soldier who's been in battle. It might cause a flashback or panic attack.

WHO ELSE?

It makes sense that people in dangerous jobs might come to have PTSD. But what about a 911 operator who listens to terrible things on the phone every day? Or a gas station attendant who works alone at night and fears being robbed because a coworker was robbed?

Constantly watching scary news, especially on social media, can cause PTSD-like symptoms. It's good to stay informed. Just set limits. Nonstop terrible scenes can leave you feeling hopeless and upset.

If the TV and internet are overloaded with upsetting images, turn them off. Go outside and get some fresh air and sunshine. Try to get your folks to come with you. All that bad news is upsetting for them too.

WHAT ABOUT ME?

Kids can live with PTSD too. There are a lot of scary things happening in the world right now. Some of them, like school shootings, affect kids.

PTSD can also be caused by things that don't get as much news coverage. Kids who live in an unstable or abusive home are at risk. So are kids who've been in an accident or have a very ill family member. Someone who feels alone or different is more likely to be diagnosed with depression, anxiety, or PTSD.

Peer Counseling

Some schools have peer counseling programs. Many kids are more comfortable talking to another teen instead of an adult. Peer counselors are older students who are good listeners. They're trained to know when something is serious enough to involve an adult.

Everyone needs someone to talk to. You can help by being a good friend. For example, try asking that kid who's always alone to join your lunch table.

Chapter 3

What Is Trauma?

I never used to worry about getting sick. Heck, sometimes I'd try to fake having a cold so I could stay home and watch TV. Now? I don't think I'll ever fool around about being sick again.

My mom and I spent a whole year hardly leaving our house because of COVID-19, and months after that wearing masks whenever we did go out. I went to school on the computer. I didn't get to hang out with any of my friends. My friend's dad died, and they couldn't even have a funeral.

My mom says it's safer—now that we're **vaccinated**—and that life must go on. I know she's right, but I still remember being scared that anyone who came near me might make me sick.

Isolation, worry, and stress over a long period of time can be harmful. Doctors will be studying the mental issues caused by the **pandemic** for many years.

TYPES OF TRAUMA

Medical doctors use the word trauma to refer to very bad injuries. Traumatic injuries take a long time to heal. They might require **surgery** or physical (bodily) therapy. They might even cause someone to live with a disability.

Counselors or psychologists use the word trauma to refer to a bad experience that takes a long time to recover, or heal, from. A traumatic experience might also involve physical injury or illness.

People who have experienced both types of traumas require special help to get better.

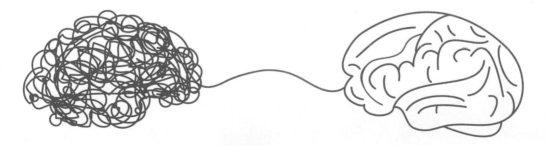

Fast Fact

A psychologist is someone whose job is to help people handle mental health problems.

It can take a long time to recover from a physical injury. Sometimes emotional injuries take just as much time and therapy; sometimes they need more.

COLLECTIVE TRAUMA

Some events are so horrible that they affect many people. When many people share an emotional response to a terrible event, it's called a collective trauma. Collective traumas include **terrorist** attacks and global pandemics.

These events affect the people involved and those who witnessed them. When an event receives lots of media coverage, even people far away are affected. They might be angry about the people who caused the event. They might also be scared that something similar could happen to them.

Get Help

NY Project Hope is a website to help New Yorkers deal with the COVID-19 pandemic. It includes a toll-free Emotional Support Helpline. Find out more at https://mentalhealthforall.nyc.gov/services/ny-project-hope. For more information on COVID-19 visit www.usa.gov/coronavirus.

COVID TRAUMA

The COVID-19 pandemic is a collective trauma. Many people have become sick and died. People worried that they might get sick. They also worried about paying bills and buying food if they lost their job. Being cut off from friends and family made it worse.

THE 9/11 TERRORIST ATTACKS

On September 11, 2001, terrorists took over three U.S. planes, including two that crashed into the World Trade Center buildings in New York City. It was the deadliest terrorist attack in U.S. history.

The attacks affected the people who witnessed them, the first responders who tried to help, and the families that **grieved** for loved ones.

People who lived far away were affected too. The attacks were on the news all the time. Many people worried about friends and loved ones on planes that had to land in strange places.

Some people were afraid to fly for a long time. Others decided they didn't want to work in such tall buildings anymore. Studies on collective traumas such as 9/11 show they can cause conditions such as short-term anxiety, long-lasting depression, and PTSD.

It took eight months to remove all the **wreckage** from the site of the World Trade Center. It's hard for people to recover when the scene of a tragedy is right where they live and work.

Chapter 4

Getting Help

After a major incident, government and disaster **relief** agencies, or groups, provide lots of help. This can include doctors, engineers, or even soldiers to restore order. It can also include mental health workers and **crisis** counselors. Local houses of worship might also offer special prayer services or connections to counseling services.

Even if you think you're OK, it's important to talk to someone about what you've experienced. Writing or drawing pictures about your feelings might also help with coping, or dealing with, a traumatic event.

Help Is Out There!

If you're upset enough to think about hurting yourself, you need to speak to someone right away. Call or text 988 to be connected to a trained crisis counselor at any time of the day or night.

The American Red Cross

The American Red Cross provides many forms of disaster recovery, including trained crisis counselors. Find out more at www.redcross.org/get-help/disaster-relief-and-recovery-services/recovering-emotionally.html

Sometimes after a scary event, specially trained dogs help to comfort people. Who doesn't feel better after hugging a dog? Just remember, you still need to talk to a person!

HELPING YOURSELF

What if there are no official resources nearby? What if the source of your stress is in your home? What if your parents or caregivers don't think you need help? These are all tough problems.

It is important that you work with someone trained to help with PTSD if you have symptoms of this condition. However, there are also some things you can do to make yourself feel better. If scary news reports are upsetting you, unplug. Practice self-care with activities that make you feel good, whether that's taking a long walk or going for a run. Movement and fresh air will help you sleep better too. Watch a silly movie or cartoon that makes you laugh.

Is there some place peaceful you can spend time? Perhaps a library, a park, or a house of worship.

Chapter 5

Coping with PTSD

It's hard to see bad things in the world and think that you can't do anything about them. Remember, people who are alone are more likely to be diagnosed with PTSD. There are things you can do to help your family heal from a traumatic event.

Remind your folks to turn off the scary news reports. Ask if you can help prepare your favorite comfort food. (They might enjoy that too!) Maybe you can even make extra to share with a neighbor. You could also bring flowers to a **memorial** or attend a candlelight **vigil**.

Coming together for a vigil can help a community heal. Coming together as a group to change a law can help keep communities safe.

BEGINNING TO HEAL

I had a long talk with my parents about school. They said it's important for me to be with other kids, especially after all the COVID-19 isolation. They understand that I'm scared. A bunch of families are passing around a **petition** to get the school to bring in special counselors.

My folks agreed that it's scary when nearly anyone can buy a powerful gun. They said sometimes they're scared of going to the supermarket.

Then they had a great idea. We read about all the people running for office this year and picked the ones who support stronger gun control laws. We also decided to attend talk therapy together. I'm glad my folks understand how I feel and are doing something to help.

Many who have been affected by gun violence, or harm, start working to pass laws for gun control. They can find it healing to share their experience and to work to make the world more peaceful.

GLOSSARY

abuse: Any action that purposefully harms another.

combat: Active fighting especially in a war.

complicated: Hard to understand, explain, or deal with.

counselor: A person who offers support and guidance in processing emotions and problems. Counseling is providing support that can help people take on problems and make decisions.

crisis: A situation that has become very serious.

dangerous: Able or likely to cause injury, pain, harm, etc.

diagnose: To recognize an illness or condition by its signs and symptoms.

disaster: Something (such as a flood, tornado, fire, plane crash, etc.) that happens suddenly and causes much suffering or loss to many people.

emotional: Causing a person to feel emotion.

grieve: To show or feel sadness or grief, which is a strong sadness caused by someone's death.

interfere: To stop or slow (something). Also to make (something) slower or more difficult.

isolation: The state of being in a place or situation that is separate from others. Also the condition of being isolated.

memorial: Something (such as a monument or ceremony) that honors a person who has died or serves as a reminder of an event in which many people died.

metal detector: A machine that gives a signal when it is close to metal. It is often used to detect weapons.

neglect: To fail to take care of or to give attention to (someone or something).

pandemic: An occurrence in which a disease spreads very quickly and affects a large number of people over a wide area or throughout the world.

petition: A formal written request to a leader or government regarding a particular cause.

reaction: The way someone acts or feels in response to something that happens, is said, etc.

relief: Things (such as food, money, or medicine) that are given to help people who have lived through a war, earthquake, flood, etc.

resource: A place or thing that provides something useful.

surgery: The branch of medicine concerned with treating illnesses and injuries, especially by cutting into the body.

terrorist: A person who uses violence to scare people as a way of achieving a political goal.

therapy: The treatment of physical or mental illnesses.

tragedy: A very bad event that causes great sadness and often involves someone's death.

vaccinate: To give someone a drug to help them better fight a specific illness, such as COVID-19. Vaccinated means having taken this drug.

vigil: An event or a period of time when a person or group stays in a place and quietly waits, prays, etc., especially at night.

wreckage: Badly damaged parts of a car, building, or other item, often after it has been destroyed.

INDEX